The Magic School Bus
Inside the Human Body

By Joanna Cole   Illustrated by Bruce Degen

SCHOLASTIC INC.

New York   Toronto   London   Auckland   Sydney

The author and illustrator wish to thank Dr. Arnold J. Capute,
Associate Professor of Pediatrics, Director, Division of Child Development,
Johns Hopkins University School of Medicine, for his help in preparing this book.

ISBN 0-590-41427-5

Text copyright © 1989 by Joanna Cole.
Illustrations copyright © 1989 by Bruce Degen.
All rights reserved. Published by Scholastic Inc.
MAGIC SCHOOL BUS is a trademark of Scholastic Inc.

20 19 18 17 16   2   3   4   5/9
Printed in the U.S.A.   08

To Craig

from Joanna & Bruce

YOUR BODY IS MADE OF CELLS
by Rachel

Your body seems to be all one piece, but actually it is made of trillions of tiny pieces, called cells.

MY BODY IS MADE OF TRILLIONS OF CELLS.

SO IS MINE!

The very next day, The Friz made us do an experiment on our own bodies.

SEE YOUR OWN CELLS

Most cells are so small that we can't see them without a microscope.

① Gently scrape inside of cheek with toothpick

② Stir end of toothpick in drop of water on a slide.

③ Add a drop of Iodine Solution to color cells.

④ Look at slide under microscope. See your cells.

OOOH, WEIRD!

Then she announced that we were going on a class trip to the science museum. We were going to see an exhibit about how our bodies get energy from the food we eat.

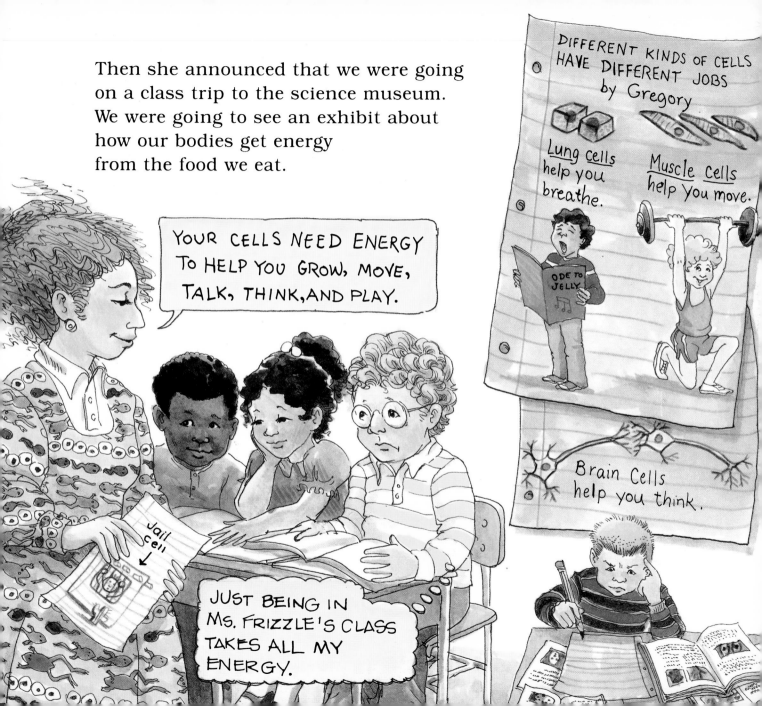

YOUR CELLS NEED ENERGY TO HELP YOU GROW, MOVE, TALK, THINK, AND PLAY.

JUST BEING IN MS. FRIZZLE'S CLASS TAKES ALL MY ENERGY.

Jail cell

DIFFERENT KINDS OF CELLS HAVE DIFFERENT JOBS
by Gregory

Lung cells help you breathe.

Muscle cells help you move.

Brain cells help you think.

YOUR TONGUE IS COVERED WITH THOUSANDS OF TASTE BUDS
        by Arnold

Different parts of the tongue have taste buds that detect different flavors.

BITTER
SOUR
SALT
SWEET

The trip started out like any other trip.
We rode to the museum
in the old school bus.
Along the way,
we stopped at a park for lunch.

LEFT OVER FISH STICKS?! ICK!

I'LL TRADE YOU THESE TERRIFIC FISH STICKS FOR THAT HORRIBLE PEANUT BUTTER AND BANANA SANDWICH.

FORGET IT!

TAKE A LOOK AT HER SHOES.

PLEASE! I'M EATING!

When it was time to go,
everyone got back on the bus—
everyone but Arnold.
He was still at the picnic table,
daydreaming and eating
a bag of Cheesie-Weesies.

WHEN YOU EAT, YOUR BODY <u>DIGESTS</u>
THE FOOD SO YOUR CELLS CAN USE IT
TO MAKE ENERGY.

YOUR BODY NEEDS
GOOD FOOD
by Carmen
For high energy and
good growing power
eat lots of:

Fresh fruits
and Vegetables

Milk and
Milk products

Whole grain
cereal and Pasta

Lean Meats, Fish,
Poultry, AND eggs

AND <u>NOT</u> TOO MUCH JUNK FOOD

A SCIENCE WORD
by Dorothy Ann

<u>Digestion</u> comes from
a word that means
to divide. When food
is digested it is divided
into smaller and smaller
parts.

"Hurry up, Arnold!" called Ms. Frizzle. She reached for the ignition key, but instead she pushed a strange little button nearby.

At once, we started shrinking and spinning through the air.

From inside, we couldn't see wha was happening. All we knew was that we landed suddenly.

and then we were going down a dark tunnel.
We had no idea where we were.
But, as usual, Ms. Frizzle knew.
She said we were inside a human body,
going down the esophagus—
the tube that leads from the throat
to the stomach.
Most of us were too upset
about leaving Arnold behind
to pay much attention.

FOOD GOES TO YOUR
STOMACH THROUGH
THE ESOPHAGUS
          by Wanda
The food does not
just fall down.
It is pushed along
by muscle actions
the way toothpaste
is squeezed out of
a tube. That's why
you can swallow even
when you are
upside down.

MUSCLES SQUEEZE
TO PUSH FOOD TO
YOUR STOMACH

WHERE'S ARNOLD?

HE GOT LEFT!

THAT'S WHAT HAPPENS WHEN YOU EAT JUNK FOOD!

I THOUGHT WE WERE GOING TO THE MUSEUM.

THERE'S BEEN A SLIGHT CHANGE OF PLANS... WE'RE BEING DIGESTED INSTEAD.

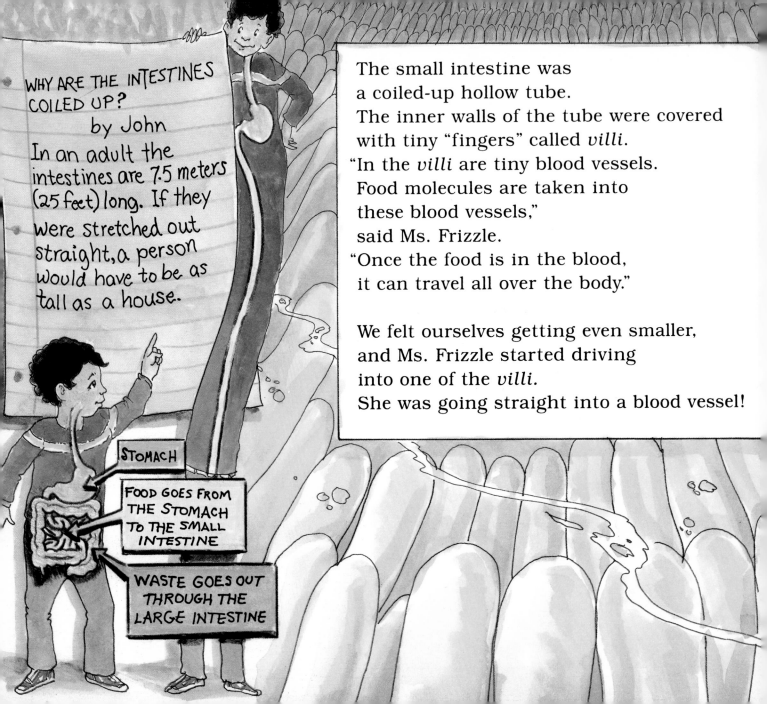

WHY ARE THE INTESTINES COILED UP?
    by John
In an adult the intestines are 7.5 meters (25 feet) long. If they were stretched out straight, a person would have to be as tall as a house.

STOMACH

FOOD GOES FROM THE *STOMACH* TO THE SMALL INTESTINE

WASTE GOES OUT THROUGH THE LARGE INTESTINE

The small intestine was
a coiled-up hollow tube.
The inner walls of the tube were covered
with tiny "fingers" called *villi*.
"In the *villi* are tiny blood vessels.
Food molecules are taken into
these blood vessels,"
said Ms. Frizzle.
"Once the food is in the blood,
it can travel all over the body."

We felt ourselves getting even smaller,
and Ms. Frizzle started driving
into one of the *villi*.
She was going straight into a blood vessel!

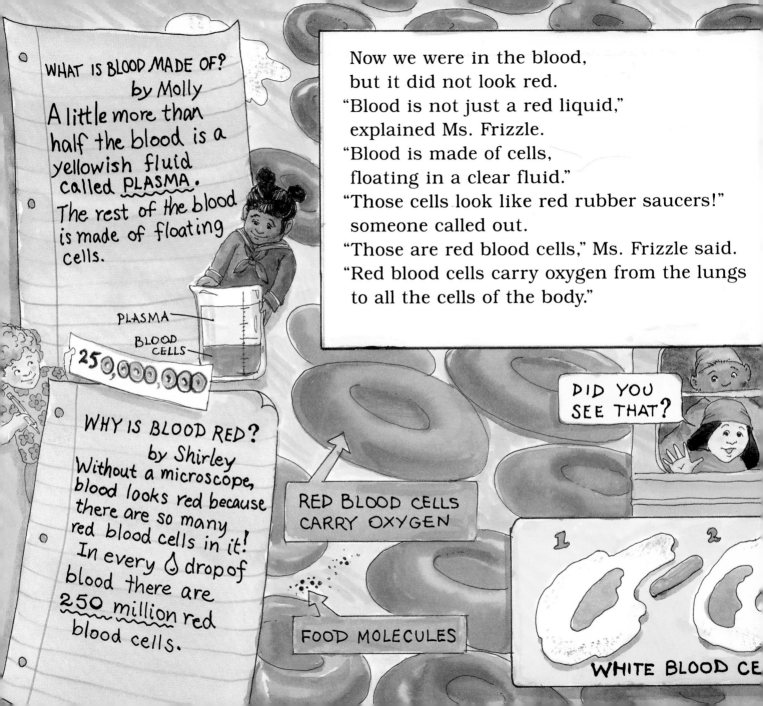

WHAT IS BLOOD MADE OF?
by Molly

A little more than half the blood is a yellowish fluid called PLASMA.
The rest of the blood is made of floating cells.

PLASMA
BLOOD CELLS
250,000,000

WHY IS BLOOD RED?
by Shirley

Without a microscope, blood looks red because there are so many red blood cells in it!
In every 🌢 drop of blood there are 250 million red blood cells.

Now we were in the blood,
but it did not look red.
"Blood is not just a red liquid,"
explained Ms. Frizzle.
"Blood is made of cells,
floating in a clear fluid."
"Those cells look like red rubber saucers!"
someone called out.
"Those are red blood cells," Ms. Frizzle said.
"Red blood cells carry oxygen from the lungs
to all the cells of the body."

DID YOU SEE THAT?

RED BLOOD CELLS CARRY OXYGEN

FOOD MOLECULES

1   2

WHITE BLOOD CE

BLOOD GOES ROUND
AND ROUND
by Michael
In less than a minute
your blood makes
a trip all around
your body.
This is called the
circulation of the
blood.

ONE MORE SCIENCE WORD
by Dorothy Ann
Circulate comes from
a word that means
"to circle". Blood
circulates - circles -
all around your body.

From the lungs, our red blood cells
carried us back to the heart.
This time we were on the left side
of the heart—the side that pumps
fresh blood back to the body again.
"Kids, it looks as if these red
blood cells are on their way to
the brain," said Ms. Frizzle.

LOOK! WHEN THE
RED BLOOD CELLS
PICK UP OXYGEN, THEY
TURN BRIGHT RED.

FROM RIGHT

AIR
SAC

When we reached the brain,
we let go of our red blood cells
and squeezed out of the blood vessel.
It was hard to believe that
this wrinkled gray blob was
the control center of the body.

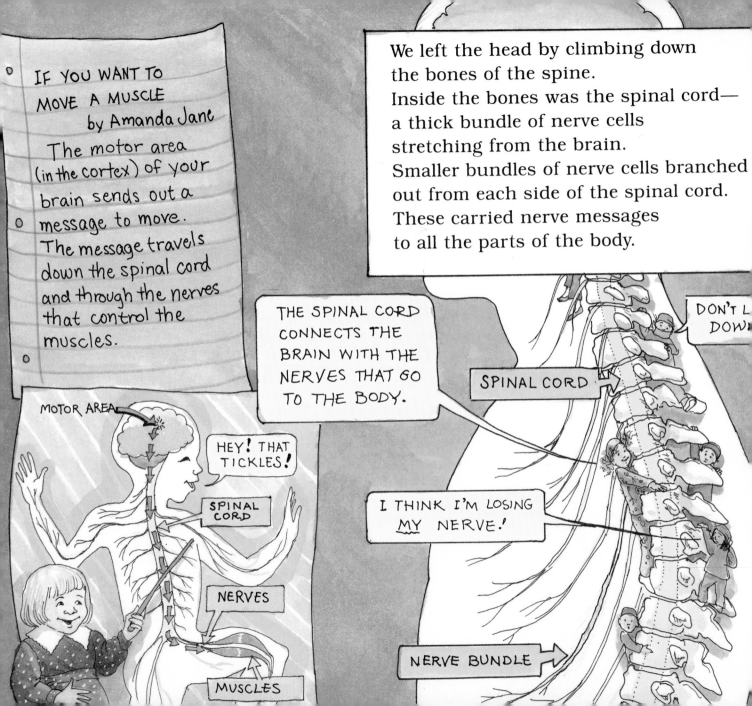

We followed some nerves that went to the leg muscles.
The leg muscles were working hard.
They needed a lot of energy.
They used up a lot of food and oxygen from the blood.
The heart was beating faster to carry fresh blood to the muscle cells.

MUSCLES MOVE YOUR BONES
by Tim

Some muscles are attached to bones. When the muscles contract (get shorter) they pull on the bones. That makes the bones move, and then you more.

MUSCLES BONES

ILDREN, WE ARE SLIDING
A MUSCLE. FROM HERE,
E'LL RETURN TO THE
LOODSTREAM.

NERVE ENDING

MUSCLE FIBER

I'LL GET THERE SOONER IF I RUN! (PANT! PANT!)

I WONDER WHERE ARNOLD IS NOW.

I HAVE THE STRANGEST FEELING HE'S CLOSE BY.

THE MORE ACTIVE YOU ARE THE FASTER YOUR HEART BEATS.

THUMP THUMP

OOD VESSEL

When we emerged from the bloodstream,
we were in a huge open space.
"Where are we?" asked a kid.
Ms. Frizzle explained,
"Children, this is the nasal cavity."
"The what?" we asked.
"The inside of the nose," said The Friz.
Suddenly, we heard a deafening noise.
It sounded like "Ah-aa-aa-ah!"

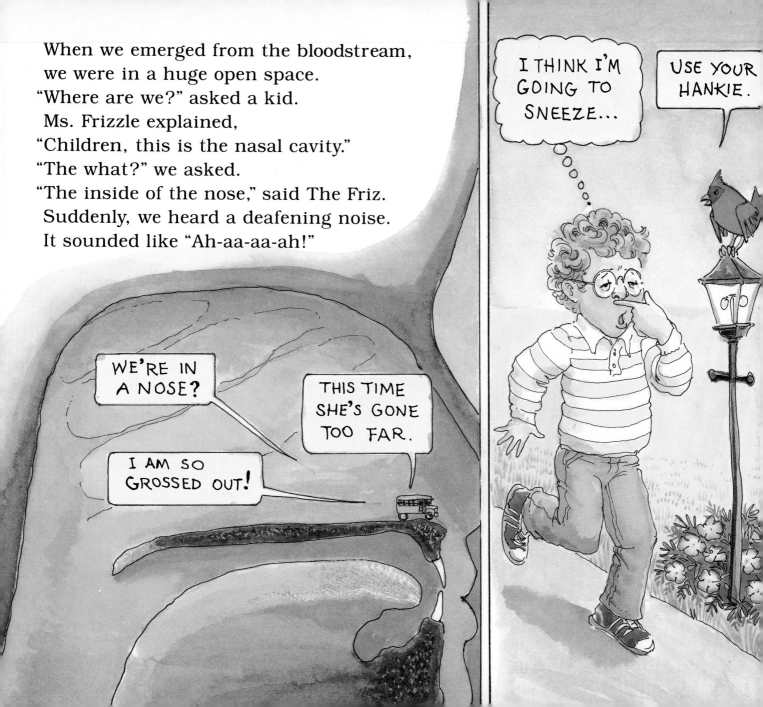

WE'RE IN A NOSE?

I AM SO GROSSED OUT!

THIS TIME SHE'S GONE TOO FAR.

I THINK I'M GOING TO SNEEZE...

USE YOUR HANKIE.

A tremendous blast of air
hit the bus full force.
We flew forward,
spinning around and around.

We were going so fast,
we couldn't see anything,
but we could tell we were getting bigger.
Then—thud!—we landed.
There we were, back at school.
And there was Arnold,
in the school parking lot,
blowing his nose.

"Arnold!" we said, "the trip was *amazing!*
You should have been there!"

Back in the classroom,
it was business as usual.
Ms. Frizzle made us draw
a chart of the human body
for the bulletin board.

THE KIDNEYS CLEAN YOUR BLOOD AND MAKE URINE.

THE BLADDER STORES URINE.

KIDNEYS

BLADDER

LIVER

STOMACH

THE LIVER STORES VITAMINS AND DESTROYS POISONS. IT ALSO MAKES BILE, A FLUID THAT HELPS DIGEST FATTY FOODS.

NERVE

BONE

TRUE-OR-FALSE TEST

STOP! TAKE THIS TEST!
DO NOT WATCH T.V.... YET.
DO NOT GET A SNACK... YET.
DO NOT PLAY A VIDEO
GAME... YET.

FIRST TAKE THIS TEST.

HOW TO:
Read the sentences below. Decide if each one is true or false. To see if you are correct, check the answers on the opposite page.

QUESTIONS:

1. A school bus can enter someone's body and kids can go on a tour. True or false?

2. Museums are boring. True or false?

3. Arnold should not have tried to get back to school by himself. True or false?

4. Children cannot breathe or talk when they are surrounded by a liquid. True or false?

5. If the children really were as small as cells, we couldn't see them without a microscope. True or false?

6. White blood cells actually chase and destroy disease germs. True or false?

7. Ms. Frizzle really knew where Arnold was the whole time. True or false?

ANSWERS:

1. False! That could not happen in real life. (Not even to Arnold.)

   But in this story the author had to make it happen. Otherwise, the book would have been about a trip to a museum, instead of a trip through the body.

2. False! Museums are interesting and fun. But they are not as weird and gross as actually going inside a human body.

3. True! In real life, it would have been safer if Arnold had found a police officer to help.

4. True. If children were *really* inside a blood vessel, they would drown. It must have been magic.

5. True! The pictures in this book show the cells and the children greatly enlarged.

6. True! As unbelievable as it seems, real white blood cells actually behave just like the ones in this book. They even squeeze through the cells of blood vessel walls to capture germs in your organs and tissues.

7. Probably true. No one is absolutely sure, but most people think Ms. Frizzle knows *everything*.

PLEASE DO NOT WRITE IN THIS BOOK.

THANK YOU.